Family as Celestial Body

poems by

Patty Ware

Finishing Line Press
Georgetown, Kentucky

Family as Celestial Body

ACKNOWLEDGMENTS

Thank you to these publications that first provided a home for the following
poems, sometimes in earlier versions or with different titles.

Cirque: "Lola"
Gyroscope Review: "Origin Story" (web site, National Poetry Month),
"Seventeen rendered portraits of my mother", "Survival of the fittest"
(originally titled "Bone")
Houston Poetry Fest Anthology (2017): "Puerta del Perdón"
Literary Mama: "Non-sequitur as metaphor"
Parentheses Journal: "Postmortem"
Slippery Elm: "Home Economics"

Publisher: Leah Huete de Maines
Editor: Christen Kincaid
Cover Art: "Bursting with stars and black holes," NASA/JPL-Caltech.
Author Photo: George Buhite
Cover Design: Elizabeth Maines McCleavy

Order online: www.finishinglinepress.com
also available on amazon.com

Author inquiries and mail orders:
Finishing Line Press
PO Box 1626
Georgetown, Kentucky 40324
USA

Table of Contents

For my family of origin, my first and most important teacher

Postmortem
after Lucie Brock-Broido

Why is family a fuzzy word. Who said
seven was a lucky number. Has he ever

answered your phone calls. Is it possible
there was trauma. Did I imagine we grew up together.

Does God play any role.

Which military base do you remember best.
Did only the girls go to Catholic schools.

Can you pinpoint
when our house began its decline.

Do you ever use the term
half-brother.

What year did we travel to the Philippines.

Did you know his father died too. Have you ever
swabbed your DNA. Why is she certain

she doesn't need therapy.
Did you hate being one of the three little ones.

Is there a nightmare that plagues you.

Which singer made mom swoon. What happens
after we die. Did dad ever bring you to the bar.

When was the last time you went to Mass. Does holding on to past
wrongs cause cancer. Can you confirm we are fixable.

How many should I set the table for.

What color have you painted your grief.
Do you think he was abused by that priest.

Is it safe to vape while wearing a canula.

Have you ever met vulnerable.

When was the last time we all danced. Is obligatory serenity
some new-age therapy technique.

In what season did mom last try to end it all.
Please share your fondest memory of our childhood.

How old were you
when you clutched your first library card.

Without peeking, what year did dad die.
Can you name our family theme song.

How good are your acting skills.

True or False: Family is a sacred chalice
or a dark room with black wire across the windows.

Home Economics

When she was ten, child of wartime
my mother trudged
seventy miles with my gram
to Cabanatuan, one skinny carabao
pulling the cart carrying everything, filled with nothing
but a small pot and wooden spoon, half sack
of rice, some dried monggo beans, bombs whumping
from the Manila they fled, my mother stopping
to pluck coconuts from trees high above her head
dashing them open
knifing milky sweetness.

When I was ten, my mother said *make two fists*
and open your arms wide then draped soft
elastic corners of a fitted queen atop knuckles lifted
like prayer, pink cotton clusters of pansies shielding
un-blossomed breasts. *Now bring your hands together*
she said, guiding my right wrist to downward curl,
fabric cupola tumbling onto my still clenched left.
Fists tight like I was being readied to fight but she instead
instructed *do the same with the other corners.*
Four fabric gables became two then one, an even line
finale'ed into tidy tight square; I asked why
we didn't fold the sheet together, and she said:
for when you are alone.

Origin story
after Rita Dove

When she was born, the sun fled despair
and earth gleamed. She was a fresh brush
waiting for permission to paint the sky.

When she was young, she sliced up sad till it bled.
There were ghosts to flee from, daydreams for delight.

She was family bound,
tongued in secrets and baptized in grief.
Blistering and blue like a bruise.

Her world already lost.
More lost than she is today.

Poem of lamentation

Her plum-colored bruises blossom
small orchids. She says it hurts
but not that much. Nothing broken.

My mother has fallen three times in four weeks.
Nothing broken. She's eighty-eight.
Such things are expected.

> My brother appointed himself
> judge, jury and executioner.
> Condemned her years ago.

Her papery skin torn in multiple places
shorn strips of flesh-colored post-its
tagging fragility. Nothing broken.

> Two of my sisters haven't spoken
> since my father's death, rocky
> fortress named grief, bluster and blast
> our family's bread and butter
>
> //push pause here//
>
> facility staff whisper
> *there's an opening in the locked unit.*

To anyone still listening, mom pleads
take me home, her ear tuned to our private recording
that plays only endings.

Dear brothers and sisters

Let's say that I keep mining. Let's say
that I hack apart our mountain.
I need to know this isn't ridiculous

rumor—the rock does shiver—
Which of you six is not
speaking to another. Who

has blocked whom
on social media.
Older sister, do you

sit in jail for landing
your hand on the back
of our younger sister.

It's impossible for me
to see gold in these
shadows. I keep

swinging, arms weary,
heavy pick above my shoulders
like when you, older brothers

used to toss me in the air.
What will become of
us, bodies wandering

tunnels riddled by family past
tattered maps in our stiff-gloved hands
muddied boots seeking exits.

Wide-eyed truth of us
hidden motherlode—I dare myself

to drop shovel.

Puerta del Perdón

(for my sisters)

I

I dreamt of us
there, karaoke bar
tables dotted with ashtrays
spilling grey-white char,
sisters swaying
back and forth
to the requested tune from
an only half attentive crowd.

We were all sassy smiles
showing off
crooked teeth,
sober enough,
belting out our theme song:
"We Are Family," harmonizing
like we were
The Andrew Sisters,
The Pointer Sisters, or even
Sister Sledge;
like we were bound
by more than blood.

II

On my Spanish
pilgrimage of prayer
I crossed the threshold
of San Isidoro's
Puerta del Perdón—
inhaled peace, unburdened
gnarled shoulders, lifted arms
heavenward. Oh, sacred moment—you,

ancient door of forgiveness
pried open
a box of joy: memories
of past zaniness
long ago asunder
ignited into blazing hue,
exploding through my
mind's eye, a brash reminder
we four sisters are
capable of grace.

Seventeen rendered portraits of my mother
after Betsy Sholl

One of my parents was a violin, the other a piano.

One suffered shrieks of unschooled strings, the other hung
suspended, a Chopin nocturne.

One was a bottle of valium with a chaser
of regret, the other a silver chalice brimming
with wisdom I was terrified to taste.

One of my parents was a bird, the other a worm.
My childhood a trail of twigs and discard—was somewhere here,
a nest?

One of my parents was a firebrand, the other a fawn
One of them I willed, the other I wept.

In the funhouse mirror of my becoming,
one song-birded her children as a blessing,
the other pinioned suffering to a cross.

Thus, my fascination with death and mystery of resurrection.

One was a middle finger, the other a genuflection.
They tried to play nice.

One was a fist, the other a prayer flag. I feared
fighting, was embarrassed I didn't know how to pray.

I was a girl running through the forest, fleeing
the sheep I mistook for a wolf.

I thought elegy was a singular noun

There are many parts, yet one body. The eye cannot say to the hand,
"I have no need of you," nor again to the feet, "I have no need of you."
(1 Corinthians, 12:20-21)

Click of tab, *FFFT of fizz;*
sure, you loved beer, it was Schlitz
every day, Schlitz all the way.

Truck driver, house painter,
cancer stick fan—you formed our family
RV from an old bread van.

You chose me, (me!) to ride
in our beige boat of a car, weekly sail
to the bar to pick up your paycheck

that smoke-filled space blurry as
a daughter's love. Slim Jims washed down
with Shirley Temples—even then I knew

our foundation hid cracks. Yet
oh, how you danced!

Jitterbug sure, skill and sway   not
impressing your sons who all chafed
at your gruff, your belt on bare asses.

Different for daughters, each swore
favorite status, we needed to
matter, auditioned for love.

We kept up our house:
patched holes and cleaned
divided windows, grappled

with faucets leaking rusted grievances
drip after drip after endless
drip.

Dear father, self-taught master
electrician and plumber, grass planter
always so certain of growth

nine years gone and our family ties
splayed, no more visits to pay, no excuses
to gather. Name us now

the House of Fracture, shards
of discord splintering hollow
doors framed by second-guesses.

Forgiveness has crept
to our table, but never stayed.

Our father—

                    deliver us.

Family as celestial body

S   I   B

N

L

G

I

asterism no longer

downward dip   once poised as plough

now loosed, unbound—tired twinkles   tilted views

from earth's adult angle

past

latched tight   tricks

of time

chanting

we were alright   expectant

as prayer. So, breathe now—

death has extinguished our Great Bear

collapse

of the core

explosion of light   impossible

to see with the naked eye

gravity binds tight
every particle of light
inside a black hole

Lola

Not American standard, not hash browns, eggs and toast but
raw chocolate unsweetened, sticky rice softened in a warm bowl.

She was *mamma* when my own mother called to her,
Lola her Tagalog name, neighborhood kids all called her gram.

We lucky true flesh grandchildren marveled at her steadfast no
to our urges for her to secure a license. Brown legs strong,

hands clutching coins, bus rides or walks fine—no need.
New birthday clothes forever unworn, coffined in boxes stashed high

at the back of her tiny brick tenement's singular closet. She grew
tomatoes and yellow squash, slick summer mugginess

of Massachusetts her adopted land when my mother
needed more hands to tend seven children in America.

Burnished beads of brown rosary wrapped in sinewy fingers
Gram sat in prayer on the stoop she shared with

Puerto Ricans and blacks, where bang, bang didn't mean
drop, hit the ground, run for cover, but slap of

screen doors closed, then opened,
then opened again and
again and
again.

D
e
m
e   a
n   i
t
                              t
              r   l
                                      e
       u   d
h
toward our
              a   l
       g   a
                    x
              y,
       c
              o   l
                        l a p
                                  s   ed

now star,   **FIERY**

ineffable

                    grace

Non-sequitur as metaphor

Not Alzheimer's, just dementia unspecified
said the neurologist, as if it were less than—
like the tiny mustard seed the Lord said becomes
the greatest of shrubs, branches into
a tree, limbs stretched skyward.

Ravens that resemble words flee from
this towering spruce, ventriloquist birds
that mew like cats, throw me off kilter
like the rotund hummingbird my mother asserts
is swollen with babies; when I tell her birds lay eggs
she laughs—*unless she's independent and wants
to do it her own way—like me!*

Honor thy mother

I

Womb-chained birther of seven
no discernable accent, shape shifter
landed by a man you knew just twenty-one days
before donning the white dress, trusting
that battle-grey ship of G.I.'s departing Manila Bay
thirty-four days retching
mestiza from a land overflowing
with less than.

II

You were different from other mothers
my oldest brother's last name you explained
came from his father, not the same
as ours, the man carving after church
ham who ferried you to this land
of plenty.

III

I asked if you were in love—
How could I be
in just twenty-one days.
So matter of fact,
your sigh, that shrug—
it seemed like it might be a nice opportunity.

IV

Rarest Vanda Sanderiana, to me everything
exotic: raised in the Philippines
in a convent for half breeds,
schooled by nuns who didn't believe
girls should know about sex
didn't welcome you back after the dashing
Filipino knocked you off kilter
inflicting the cross you mistook
for love.

V

You learned to blend in to American
life, cook and clean, kiss children goodnight
obedient wife for a man who liked
his drink. Meek as an un-touched
peach, you dreamt of
drowning or was it sweet
lure of ripeness?

VI

You assured me there was no such thing—
the man who made me swoon was not a man
who would take care of me—*you won't find them
in the same package*, you said, as if
men were frozen entrees, their traits encased
in separate tins, medleys not included.
You spent your life searching
for proof, seeking the truth of this
self-spun theorem, man, after man, after
man.

VII

Kitchen-warrior, goddess of Sinigang,
all that I know tucked tight inside your years
viscous like the drip of pork fat—
the way it clung to dad's metal screen
strainer built snug over our sink
to welcome your filling—wrapped
egg rolls by the hundreds to feed your brood.
Classical music lover, Youth Dew dauber
scholar of suffering, thrice failed student
of self-ending.

VIII

It was only after dad's death
that your befuddlement spoke, as if
in tongues: *It was him all along, I never knew
and now he's gone.* Sixty-two years
you slogged, trying to sever, then
he became sainted, finally better
than all the rest.

But this   is no judgment.

IX

It was you I called from the ER, you
who flew five thousand miles to mend me
from the hemorrhage no longer named
pregnancy, the husband no longer
named mine. You were limitless presence
on the other end of my phone line,
Gibraltar as woman born.

I miss the way your voice once tasted
the world, sweet smother of you
as love drunk grandmother, the way
you lifted each of my babies like
a benediction, each tiny body your own
second chance.

X

Our ties twist thick with the now
of forgetting, I can't understand
your consultations with angels,
but I remember the empress resplendent
in golden silk, before I beheld
her nakedness.

The unraveling

When I visit my mother and ask if
she has eaten, an uproarious cackle unspools

> before I am baptized by her dead-
> panned *you can laugh all you want*

which is unsettling because I am not
laughing and there's her raucous cry, its sharp black night

> as if she is hugging herself tight
> in one of those white jackets, straited and buckled.

Last evening, I watched a film clear to its finish—
sense of familiar nudging my mind, and when

> my chest tightened at that wimpled nun
> with slits for eyes and spit for words

> I didn't connect the dots that dragged
> memory through tunnels and

when I predicted *she'll knock on the door*

> and my husband announced *we've seen this already*

I denounced him with the vigor of a drunk

> asserting she is stone cold sober.

When I look in the mirror, I see my mother
dimly but when next I see her

> face to face, she peers into the tiny black trash bin
> filled with candy wrappers; she points into its dark cavern

they've all gathered, but they're waiting
for their drink of water.

Permission
after Farnaz Fatemi

Mother, let's fling open
the tight-lipped drapes, set free
your ghosts. We'll remove the trinity
of silver T-pins shutting up
your paisley'd life—let's not risk
tenderness—yank them loose
with a single swift tug, uncork
grenades that we can toss
toward grace.

We'll slide solid brass rings along
the rod of your past, spur them to
sing, yes, they'll sing! Songs of release
that lucky prize sometimes
granted to the mind folded back
on itself.

Feel the safe slide of silk
against our skin, part that outer layer
that refused to open, clasped as it was
against judgment. We'll reach to remove
the dingy sheers sooted with
years of apology, watch them shred
into strips, float past us.
Like words without an anchor
the nuns were so focused on saving
souls and the structure of sentences, they failed
to teach you about sex
or suicide. Dear mother, forgiveness
didn't find you hiding
in a confessional. The split
curtains will gaze at each other
from opposite sides of the window
and dance.

Survival of the fittest
(for Emily)

As a girl, I never heard the word
patriarchy, was taught to fear feminists who nurtured

armpit nests, named themselves in shorthand
clipped and cool, Sid or Sal.

Her name flowered my tongue, her words
slipped like silk onto my skin, she spoke of

stolen dreams, of a self that the system subverted, strength
severed, rose snipped, placed in a vase to be gazed upon
body shimmering like a thorn.

She said it soft before she swore she would no longer stay silent.
Bone, she said as if our hard, wide curve

of pelvis cradled every power
we would ever need, as if mouthing it
unshackled our strength.

Bone--not bone of my bone, not words
spilled from Adam, not Genesis proclaimed

by collared celibates preaching without irony
of marriage—that melding of flesh and heart
and yes, bone—no

hers was the bone of breath, bone that girdles womb
our womb that widens, unafraid to yield

bone that births without preference
for female or male—hard bone, bone of resistance

spirit bone, bone of salt
bone of flame, bone of fist
bone of acceptance, bone of gift.

Bury a bone, compress it, drown it
in sediment and it becomes rock.

My bone is flint—strike.

With Gratitude

I offer immense gratitude to my first writing group, Juneau's Burn Thompson Group, for teaching me how it's done; to Total Immersion Group for challenging me to become a better poet; to Mistee St. Clair for her mentorship, friendship and insistence that I was a good enough writer for this to happen; and to my husband George, who bore with unfailing patience each and every revision he had to listen to, gently letting me know when something "didn't quite work."

Proceeds from the sale of this chapbook will be donated to 49 Writers, an Alaska literary organization dedicated to creativity, community and craft, from which Patty benefited via retreats, workshops and classes. Though she now lives in Portland, these poems were written in Alaska, her forever home.

Patty Ware has been a waitress, shoe salesperson, Peace Corps volunteer, substance abuse counselor, foster care coordinator, and Juvenile Justice Director, but her most important roles have been those of mother, grandmother, wife, sister, daughter, and friend. She moved to Portland Oregon in the fall of 2024 to be closer to family after spending most of her life in Juneau, Alaska. She holds a BA in Psychology from Amherst College and an MPA from the University of Alaska, Southeast.

www.ingramcontent.com/pod-product-compliance
Lightning Source LLC
Chambersburg PA
CBHW022101080426
42734CB00009B/1449